The Deadly Shadow
of the Wall

poems by

R. W. Haynes

Finishing Line Press
Georgetown, Kentucky

The Deadly Shadow of the Wall

Copyright © 2022 by R. W. Haynes
ISBN 979-8-88838-029-1 First Edition
All rights reserved under International and Pan-American Copyright Conventions.
No part of this book may be reproduced in any manner whatsoever without written permission from the publisher, except in the case of brief quotations embodied in critical articles and reviews.

ACKNOWLEDGMENTS

The following poems previously appeared as indicated below. My thanks to the respective editors for their kind consideration.

"Thinking Doesn't," *Abridged* (Northern Ireland), "Nyx," December 21, 2020.
"Carpet Page for Vernacular Watercraft," *Lothlorien Poetry Journal* (Scotland), April 2021.
"Saludos from a Grateful Mind (Slightly Demented Now by Prophetic Strain)," and "Collecting Hot Checks for the Redneck Diaspora," *DREICH* 7, Season Two (Scotland), April 2021.
"Another Ha Ha Chuckle for the Blessing of Rest," "Mrs. Alving Contemplates Her Nipples," "Like Epictetus on Mushrooms," *Poetry Life & Times* (UK), October 2021.
"Slap that Mosquito, Phaedrus, My Friend," *ZIN Daily* (Croatia), October 2022.

Publisher: Leah Huete de Maines
Editor: Christen Kincaid
Cover Art: Ruth Yolanda Haynes
Author Photo: Ruth Yolanda Haynes
Cover Design: Elizabeth Maines McCleavy

Order online: www.finishinglinepress.com
also available on amazon.com

Author inquiries and mail orders:
Finishing Line Press
P. O. Box 1626
Georgetown, Kentucky 40324
U. S. A.

Table of Contents

In the Deadly Shadow of the Wall 1
The Shades of Quality 2
Two Kinds of Flight 3
Eye Contact Onstage 4
But Thinking Doesn't 5
Ballad: What Every Child Should Know 6
Don't Look at Me 7
Fatal Sculptress Defends Her Boyfriend to Her Mother 8
Carpet Page for Vernacular Watercraft 9
Kind Wish for Quiet 10
A Well-Intended Imperative 11
Did Your Muse Really Say 12
Touching Up the Cure for Love 13
The Smoldering Ashes of the Monastery 14
Dire Wolf Devours Whole Sack of Puppy Chow 15
Elective Affinities in the Poodle Dog Lounge 16
Escape to Alexandria 17
Father Hopkins's Trappist Twin Makes a Few Notes 18
To the Girl Who Grew Old from the Boy Who Didn't 19
Jaques in Love 21
A.D. 2019: Principled Conservative Designs Stainless
    Hygienic Toddler Cage 22
If You Love Me, Believe Me, Frogs Never Lie 23
Stairwell Wisdom's Low High Tide 24
The Sonnet Named "Don't Trust Sleep" 25
Name No One Man, Bob 26
Saludos from a Grateful Mind (Slightly Demented Now
    by Prophetic Strain) 27
Collecting Hot Checks for the Redneck Diaspora 28
Emily Dickinson Writes to a Young Poet in Texas 29

A Mile from the River 30
Dr. Bradford Views David's "The Death of Socrates" 31
History Makes No Difference to Me 32
Lobster-Stuffed Possum with Dill Mayonnaise 33
Foot-Washing Baptist Mourns for Beirut 34
The Happy, Aporetic, Apotropaic Laugh 35
Middle-Aged Lovers on Culebra Avenue 36
Stella Adler Tells Her Grandfather Clock How to Tick 37
Good Provider Loses His Ass at the Chicken Fights 38
Another Ha Ha Chuckle for the Blessing of Rest 39
Mrs. Alving Contemplates Her Nipples 40
Like Epictetus on Mushrooms 41
The Vigor of Our Cloud-Hidden Friend 42
Let Decrepitude Run the Table 43
Elderly Cassandra Foresees that the Orderly Cleaning Her
    Backside Will Someday Write Poetry about Waco 44
Song of the Cabbage Head 45
Mr. Poe Extends a Mexican Invitation 46
Academic Couple #1760 47
Call Me Inconsiderate, Honey 48
Fourteener for the Busy Bee 49
Troubled Stoic Deletes Favorite Pancake Recipe 50
Héloïse and Abelard Dissolve in the Student Center Cafeteria 51
Fresh Water Jellyfish Head for the Rapids 52
New Orleans: The Reparations for Prohibition 53
Prince Myshkin Bets on Being Prepared 54
Slap That Mosquito, Phaedrus, My Friend 55
Roman Mosaic Predicts Texas Cadillac Ranch 56
Sola Scriptura Hits the Home Stretch 57
Mrs. Collins on Ritual and Routine 58
A Light Blues for Aphasia 59
Camping in the Rain 60

For Ruthie

In the Deadly Shadow of the Wall

Ἀμηχανία, "goddess of helplessness"

Lack of dialogue is an essential form
Of the elusive indeterminate dyad;
Neither single nor double, nor cold nor warm,
It manifests itself in voyages I had
Toward delusions of an Ithacan dream,
And, now, in mathematical consolation
For plans shot to hell and floating downstream,
I relish the justice of half-assed devastation.
If I were in a honky-tonk, slurping up beer,
Hearing fake rednecks yodeling fake pain,
I couldn't do the math as I can do here,
Or realize arithmetic, now, makes love plain.
As the ravens fly across a white background
I focus to re-calculate the solution I found.

The Shades of Quality

Blood pressure rises and intelligence declines.
I need a stupidometer that will connect
A blood pressure gauge to my poetic lines
To show by the color of the text a direct
Indication of my hydraulic state
At the time of composition, so when I seem
Unduly foolish, the reader can relate
That incapacity to the impeded stream
Of oxygen-bearing blood from the splurging heart:
"The text is orange here, so we must not expect
The kind of quality found in the green part
Reflecting rhythm of heart and intellect."
This invented, no one has to curse
Tangerine passages afflicting this verse.

Two Kinds of Flight

The dart flies toward the dartboard, which mutates
Into a houseful of loved ones, innocent
Of anything deserving what you just sent,
And sometimes the dart merely stimulates
Hilarity, proving all you do is funny,
Well-intentioned, although prone to blunder,
Meant to fly, but always crawling under,
To prosper, oh, but always losing money.
But sometimes the playful arrow's homeward flight
Strikes a brother, sometimes spontaneity
Strikes shot and shooter devastatingly,
Submerging the spirit in remorseful night.
We launch forth these liberated birds,
And they fly away like wild and frenzied words.

Eye Contact Onstage

Eye contact onstage can be a mistake,
But one cannot act without this connection
Or represent delight or fatal heartbreak
With eyes aimed off in some obtuse direction,
So the actor rolls the dice and frankly gazes
Into the lying eyes he meets in plays,
Praying inwardly the thoughts this raises
Belong to the character that he conveys.
Collapsing in hysterics never pays,
Unless that is directed for the part,
And risks financial parting of the ways
And banishment from the histrionic art.
Those not actors can ignore these rules
And play Antigone and Oedipus as fools.

But Thinking Doesn't

Thinking doesn't create time unless
Pain kicks in to clinch the deal,
Driving love through rafters, scantlings,
Scaring fierce old cats from their thrones,
Smug old memories from their feather beds,
Lazy comfort from its leather couch,
Waking little desperate quartets of faith,
Hope, all-but-abandoned love, panic,
Jolts of panic as a vast flock of owls
Sees the light, feathers like a mob,
Choking the darkness with silent wings,
Threatening light itself, frightening
The very crazy idea of light, click.

Ballad: What Every Child Should Know

When you lift an eyebrow
In scorn or apathy,
Pray for the terrified sailors
You're drowning in the sea.

Storms emerge from facial expressions,
Their treason blown up by hidden deceit,
And in their forcible retrogressions
Disguise explodes as it grows complete.

How do you like those pirates, Tyrone,
Roguish and jolly, banes of the sea?
They've lost their terror and now have grown
Into saltwater comics, no danger to me,

Not when the clouds climb past constellations
And whirl into massively nightmarish blast,
And madness screams death, insane invocations,
And future is crushed in the jaws of the past.

When you lift an eyebrow
In scorn or apathy,
Pray for the terrified sailors
You're drowning in the sea.

Don't Look at Me

Fangs, drool, splintering bones, shrieks,
You can't hide here; they'll get us all,
And mercy doesn't jump in when you call.
Heavy footsteps approach, the floor squeaks.
You put down that stupid volume of crap
And thought a clever voice from a sad past
Might entertain like a bittersweet blast
But now you face this final hideous trap,
Grim and greedy, mortal, your nightmare
From that dark, dangerous, destructive place
Where poetry rips off your foolish face
And cuts you, leaves you staggering there.
I tried to warn you, tried stumblingly,
But love just smirked and said "Don't look at me."

Fatal Sculptress Defends Her Boyfriend to Her Mother

"He liked my *Medusa*. He said he thought
The Snoring Odysseus witty and profound,
But you don't like it when he comes around,
And you don't remember those dahlias he brought.
I'm twenty-three, you know, and he may be
Different from what you and Dad prefer,
But I love him; a woman knows what's best for her,
And he understands what sculpture means to me.
When he saw *Dido's Rapture* he gave such a smile
It lit up my heart, and *Medea's Goodbye*
Brought forth a truly passionate sigh,
And he stared at it for a long, long while.
His warm imagination and sympathetic heart
Mean nothing can ever keep us apart."

Carpet Page for Vernacular Watercraft

I only drink water just before I drown,
Grinned the old man with the too-bright eyes.
Never put out a fire before it dies
Or go to a funeral with a sober clown.

Here I have it easy; my only sorrow
Is that my dogs will wonder where I went
And miss the morning treats their angels sent
When I kick the sun tomorrow.

Be careful with love, always respect
The lady of Cyprus, whose deadly might
Will wrap you up in a knot so tight
You'll never get to sleep at night,
Eaten internally for bitter neglect.

Give her honor; pass on one side
If possible, give a discreet shake
Of your bells, for love's sweet sake,
And never assume her power has died.

I only drink water just before I drown,
Grinned the old man with the too-bright eyes.
Never put out a fire before it dies
Or go to a funeral with a sober clown.

Kind Wish for Quiet

If the mental convulsions of the obtuse
Deserve a moment of Olympian disdain,
Let that justice tolerate some pain
As that indulgent art runs loose.
If some mute inglorious Milton strains,
Celebrating moments of dull-felt rapture
Only the aphasiac can capture,
Let him enjoy unleashing his brains.
We are all called to different tasks, each one,
Some to rule, some to overrule,
Some to drool, and some to play the fool,
But all at last sink like the setting sun.
Let your charms set you absolutely free
To drowse among your gods contentedly.

A Well-Intended Imperative

> *But when the admirals came and gave their divers votes at the altar of Poseidon, to judge who was first and who second among them, each of them there voted for himself....*
> Herodotus VIII.123 (Godley tr.)

> *"Fair" died with the Easter Bunny.*
> Mahulda M. McDonald

Go home to yourself and find therein
A blessed rest enabling you to be
Yourself in quiet spirituality
Unvexed by my voice, my mandolin.
A timely silence fills the heart with peace,
And timely absence soothes the battered soul,
And time brings timely hope its quiet goal,
As dying storms at last bring sweet release.
The old stuff died. Its bitter consequence
Evaporates like fast-plucked notes you heard
As introductions to a parting word
Thrown out to dramatize some hot nonsense.
Peace, then. If I can give that now,
I'll try at length to get my share somehow.

Did Your Muse Really Say

Did your Muse really say," Rough South, my ass?"
Can't you get anything under control at all?
Your market has collapsed far beyond recall
And time, reeling and rocking, continues to pass.
When you reached for whiskey and sang aloud
Like a halfwit Catullus to glorify beauty
As though hysterics were the bard's fatal duty,
Was that all right, man? Was that allowed?
Let's talk about broken hearts, shall we, Jim?
Or maybe lost money, or long-dead pets,
Or humiliation, or self-destructive bets,
And think of Shakespeare, and tell our tale to him.
And when our prayer comes back down from the stars,
Let's grind our teeth and tune our old guitars.

Touching Up the Cure for Love

Let's say all that Romantic stuff is true,
And, as I put my fishing stuff in the car,
You contemplate all that, and what we are,
And where we'll go when classes all are through.
Do I lie enough, or have you finally found
The numerous bodies buried underground,
Rotten skeletons, the happy worms' playground?
And all those bloody-hoarded gold doubloons,
Rusty cutlasses, bejeweled mugs,
Old skulls populated now by bugs,
All cursed by Hate under midnight moons?
Touch up your make-up, dear, and reflect
That sacking cities no longer is correct:
The heroes today *are* the slobbering buffoons.

The Smoldering Ashes of the Monastery

Why say that I capitulated to
The forces of avarice and of that envy
Time let accumulate against me?
Was there something more heroic to do
Than ignore any advantages proposed
As well as the blustery intimidation?
The hot theater of self-identification
Cooled long ago, as fantasies, exposed
To the withering light of the noonday sun,
Surrendered to sanity; the vessel ran ashore,
Plunder exhausted, the magic sword I bore,
The last glowing force of desperation.
To organize for the last contention,
Is the last and best devastation prevention.

Dire Wolf Devours Whole Sack of Puppy Chow, Shakes Stuffed Bear Like Rat

Most sweet of lovely ladies, the troubadour sang,
Nerve of my verve, my heartbeat's harmony,
Thou art the blast of blessing, the bell that rang
In Heaven's secret chapel of divinity,
I pray thy mercy, one all-redeeming glance
From Aphrodisian eyes, whose heavenly glow
Can banish harm and nourish love to grow
And desperation itself rejoice and dance.
His sonnet interrupted, Muse given pause,
He shakes his head, "Have I awoken
Before my magic spell was fully spoken?
Will that old wolf now grab me in his jaws
And chomp me up like I was puppy chow?
Stand back, my dear, I have to fight him now."

Elective Affinities in the Poodle Dog Lounge

I was trying to remember who did that old
Blues song celebrating some poor guy
Whose lady one day left him high and dry,
Robbed a liquor store, and left him in the cold.
And then somebody called my name out clear,
But I passed out and never saw her face,
But I still wonder about that shady place
And how the hell I got from there to here.
Was it you, dead Gloria, or you, Lily Bell,
Or Queen Elizabeth, of glorious fantasy,
Calling out so urgently to me,
To say, here's Heaven, come leave this Hell?
Memory can be sordid: one has to scrounge
In dim recollection of the Poodle Dog Lounge.

Escape to Alexandria

Thistle blue in abandoned land,
However small that urgent hope may be,
It has its own concentrated force,
And, like young love disdained by fools,
It will outlast the worst hostility.
Your faith on that, Cleopatra, when
Your showboat steams like a coastal squall
Across this Atchafalayan dream,
Cargado de oro for fools without sense,
Banners like lingerie from old Istanbul,
Your face printed in a confident smile,
Scents of raw passions enriching the breeze,
A thrill even now for a man of many turns,
"Well, when I first saw my baby, y'all,
I was headin' to the bank.
An' when I last saw my baby, oh,
I was headin' to the tank."

Thistle blue under a cloudy thundery sky,
When hope fades back, you know it's still alive,
And some Egyptian boat is bringing things
To tantalize your mind, so nature plays,
And, bitter as you are, you lick your chops
And ask for cards, and somewhat wearily smile,
And wait for passionate news from up the Nile.

Father Hopkins's Trappist Twin Makes a Few Notes

It was good of Coleridge to take us to
The shenanigans in Xanadu,
But he woke up before he was through,
Unfortunately for me and you.

Yes, ladies and gentlemen,
Poetry can evaporate when
Distracted Muses leave us to spin
In frantic hope they'll connect again.

Take your regular medicine for pain
And, in a few hours, why, take another,
Otherwise agony will drive you insane,
And none of us wants that, do we, brother?

Put new strings on your banjo at times,
Make a little speech and see if it rhymes,
Tap dance ten minutes before you sleep,
Pray for the wolves, and pray for the sheep,
The lies you tell, the promises you keep.

To the Girl Who Grew Old from the Boy Who Didn't

Magic can be hell, but, generally,
It glides along like a silent hawk, perceives
Everything, but passes by and leaves
Us drowsily sure we're magic-free.
That's why she grew aged, while he,
Munching on a ten-dollar ice cream cone,
Skipped that inconvenience magically,
As he stood stock-still, and she went on.
He pulled a Dylan, told her "Fare thee well,"
And climbed aboard his creaky little cart,
And drove off to lonely lands of art,
And left behind his loud-protesting heart,
But he showed her, by God, that he meant well.
So he stayed young and foolish: there he stands,
Shaking colored gourds, rattling in his hands.

        Radiating a kind of bitter goodwill
        I look across from my dome in the sky
        And extend this figurative goodbye,
        Believing that you will fare well until
        Silver raindrops and emerald hail
        Swirl into a sweet-honeyed storm
        And puppies and kittens come scampering to warm
        Their magical queen—hail! All hail!
        Permit this presumption; at least I've earned
        That much, and still haven't learned
        The bare-bones discretion Epictetus taught,
        Which once seemed perfect, as I then thought,
        A magical cure for heroes badly burned.
        One forgets how these illusions end…
        Oho, how well you hid your smiling friend.

The truth is in the desert—though these dramatic
Lovers, if that's what they should be called,
In one-way love here were awkwardly stalled—
Out where starving saints became fanatic,
And the stage is simple for love's true play,

For death plays a hard fiddle under the sun
And stagy emotions are soon outrun
And dry and vanish as dreams pass away.
All the tricks and promises treasured before
When golden Aphrodite extended her hands
Become silly memories in these hard lands
And no longer tempt the heart any more.
The stage of love has pleasures, delusive as fear,
But today we find love's struggling truth here.

Jaques in Love

I was thinking that just the right parody
Would lay my mind to rest about events
That now devour that nice tranquility
Treasured once and longed for ever since.
And, tuning up for that satirical strain,
Why, all at once, my cocky, confident wit
Vanished, blasted—a disconcerting train
Of gloomy images just overwhelmed it.
Poverty of thought evokes no grace
But that which humiliation brings,
Inviting injustice to show its ugly face
Forbidding erasure of these painful things.
A fool's parody works for others' pleasure
When silence demands its rightful measure.

Anno Domini 2019: Principled Conservative Designs Stainless Hygienic Toddler Cage, Awarded Presidential Medal of Freedom

No, Minnie, I told my husband there was no doubt
Them astronauts was causin' all that rain,
And Fox News made it clear the news was out:
Old Elvis has a bungalow in Spain,
And there he lives, with Jackie's missing twin,
And Darth Vader, and them he rescued high and dry
From Gilligan's Island, away back when
The Navy wouldn't lift a hand to try.
No, what we need in this world today
Is get up and go, not got up and went,
And bidness knowledge, whatever you may say,
And the line-item veto on whatever gets spent.
If we let bidnessmen have a free hand,
We'll see prosperity return to the land.

If You Love Me, Believe Me, Frogs Never Lie

Let me consider righteous indignation
Not sanctimonious irritation
But rather that it somehow organizes
That sometimes messy internal location
Where we are distracted by surprises
And lose our grip on patient toleration.
When it evaporates before reflection,
We grow in wisdom, a while, at least,
And briefly forget that ferocious beast
Of rage that waits, just beyond detection.
So sometimes, when the famous fat lady sings,
We sigh to think our stress will have an end,
Yet while we meditate and try to mend,
We still hear echoes of malicious things.

Stairwell Wisdom's Low High Tide

Here is the latest stimulating headline.
Scientists find ultimatums backfire,
Accusations flop, jeers expire.
No need to go to India, friends of mine.
No need to analyze excessively
The tranquil landscapes of pastoral peace,
For horror hides everywhere, awaits release,
And too many questions tend to set it free.
Fear, however, a fairly sorry force,
Must not tyrannize our pleasure here,
So when prudence can extinguish fear,
Let timely wisdom choose that easy course.
Slogans, headlines, formulas, and clichés:
These devices lubricate our dull days.

The Sonnet Named "Don't Trust Sleep"

Don't trust sleep, wherever you travel:
If the cat whispers something treacherous
As the moon ducks crazy, hell-bent crows,
And silence, otherwise, looms, looms and grows,
Wait for the waterfall's growl down its precipice,
And a dead man's footsteps crunching the gravel.
He taught her to play a suspicious slide guitar.
She taught him to doubt everything he heard.
They lived like two wolves and howled at the skies
Where the red foxes hide and the black owl flies,
At times not exchanging much more than a word,
Within savage silence where the great spaces are.
Oh, yes, you know all this, you see through faces,
And smile a bit as I go through my paces.

Name No One Man, Bob

So thus it was. You sweetly wept a bit
As Juliet crashed her little plastic bike,
And the old chatterboxes cackled like
Mixed-up market geese confused by it.
"Yeah, sure, let's do some statues of gold, old boy,
To show Verona's folk how cool we are,
And rich, although we took the feud too far,
And blew old age, and fucked up family joy."
But I liked how in Juliet's sweet bravery
You found yourself, and would have died that way
If you'd awakened in that tomb one day
And found yourself beside someone like me.
Sweetness of a kind grows and survives
In good old plays and in some sinful lives.

Saludos from a Grateful Mind
(Slightly Demented Now by Prophetic Strain)

Thank you for coming to my doctoral defense
And bringing clouds of calmness to the mess.
I thought with gratitude and happiness
I'd try to compensate your common sense,
For that is central to all poetry,
As you knew better then than I conceived,
Although back then there were times I believed
That no new knowledge lay in wait for me.
Why do I still enjoy so much today
How you held forth on Tintern Abbey then,
And, as I think of Old Wordsworth again,
Smile stupidly as his iambs replay?
I don't know much of anything any more,
Perhaps, but that I kindly thank you for.

Collecting Hot Checks for the Redneck Diaspora

Why doesn't someone teach these folks
You can't do literature if all you want to do
Is think up clever crap and claim it's new?
Poems fall like thunder when the keyboard smokes.
Well, yesterday, I smoked half a dozen hogs,
And plowed a half a mile of rocky ground
And played the fiddle some, and put it down,
And howled for supper louder than the dogs,
And some mean-looking woman on TV
Declared that guys like me should disappear,
But when she's gone, God knows we'll still be here
And show how strong chthonic gods can be.
Hold on, goat-ropers, till I get this right,
And get my fiddle-tuning halfway tight.

Emily Dickinson Writes to a Young Poet in Texas

You can't let your poems own you, dear,
Or there will be disturbance in your heart
You cannot manage. Set the scraps apart
Like shoes that simply served to bring you here.
The passions driving poems are your own
As long as you can tidy them away
To have their shock at hand another day
Unwithered by the scorn of what you've shown,
Seasoned by survival as hope has grown.
Let that hope go skirting with a critic
And loss of self goes with it, willy-nilly,
And decoration wrecks you, silly-frilly,
Swollen, bug-eyed, crazed, and paralytic.
Bloom apart in strength, a lonely lily.

A Mile from the River

The house full of books isn't going anywhere,
And the dog and I step out with vigorous hope
For cats and peace of mind. We're leashed
To great expectations as we pace
Down Rancho Viejo toward the Rio Grande.
He knows where all the carping dogs
Reside on this street, and has an answer
For each of them. If he were loose,
He'd murder them all, he muses,
But duty calls, and his master needs
A steady pull upon the leash
To keep from getting lost.

Dr. Bradford Views David's "The Death of Socrates"

History radiates from moments such as these,
And old time is forestalled in his revolutions
By your brush, and Socrates is to be dragged
Kicking and screaming, as it were, away
From Athens and into your own nightmare,
From tepid hemlock to razor-sharp guillotine,
And Plato, or Pluto, as one of my students wrote,
Left in silence at the foot of the bed,
Revolving his volatile, contagious ideas.
If I may suggest one anachronism more,
Add Honest Abe's Bible to the things on the floor.

History Makes No Difference to Me

"History makes no difference to me,"
She said, tying her scarf under her chin,
Picking up her umbrella and her bag,
And stopping to look me in the eye,
"I have too much on my mind right now.
I hope you understand, and I'll call tonight."
If, or when, she called, I was not there,
But since history does make a difference,
I think the neatness of that knotted scarf
Made history, a dexterous farewell,
Among the bonds of dissolution
And pangs of last looks in the eye.

Lobster-Stuffed Possum with Dill Mayonnaise
(Or, You're Only Crazy If You Admit It)

It's normal for idiots to be in control;
Ask Achilles, Hamlet, or Antigone,
Or anyone in the laughing academy:
They'll smile and tell you that's how things roll.
Being crazy is hard work, but all the cool
Respect one's expertise and wisely nod
To see you do the holy work of God
To send the sane fools back to baby school.
Why, let's have dinner, let the greasy chips
Fall where they must, where the waiting hounds
Wait and lick, quick for the rebounds,
As food goes in and words go out our lips.
And following dinner's tremendous violence
Here comes dessert! An explosive silence.

Foot-Washing Baptist Mourns for Beirut

Blame doesn't always cut it. One sees
A slackness of duty everywhere, and this
Fault plagues me. I invariably miss
Important calls, responsibilities,
And here I am, helpless on my knees,
Shaken up, but this paralysis
Blew us all to anagnorisis,
Explosion adding terror to disease.
Oh, my Lord, in my sense
I'm just smoldering fragments
Burned by my brothers' love of ease.
Rain on us now with blessed rain
That kills nothing else but mindless pain.

The Happy, Aporetic, Apotropaic Laugh

Let me give credit where it's due
And commemorate a moment I recall
When poor old Wile E. Coyote hit the wall
And how his mighty crash amused you.
"He reminds me of you," you laughed and said,
"Chasing his enemy with death in his eye
And then his own dynamite blows him sky-high,
And he comes back with a new trick instead."
"Laugh, woman, laugh," was my reply,
And she did. I hope that she is laughing still:
In Athens or Rome, may her laughter fill
The cafés and restaurants, echo to the sky,
As pleasing to all as the memory to me.
Laugh, woman, laugh—I will smile quietly.

Middle-Aged Lovers on Culebra Avenue

Juliet: This serene and blessed mood doth provide,
 O Shakespeare, a consolation old Boethius,
 Locked in that fearsome cell before he died,
 Might graciously and bravely have wished for us
 As we jolt down this midnight street and pass
 The Culebra Meat Market, our hearts aglow
 Like cathedrals immured with radiant glass,
 Spirits content, in San Antonio.
Romeo: The demented demons have been shut out
 For the moment, and now their twisted lies
 Twist in the hopeful wind, their taint of doubt
 Feeble as their prevaricating eyes.
 And we feel this comfort, know that tonight
 Now our yoke is easy, our burden is light.

Stella Adler Tells Her Grandfather Clock How to Tick

Don't tick like that! Where does your steel
Come from? What little elf in Switzerland
Shaped your soul with magic-crafty hand?
Get rid of logic! Don't think! Just feel
How clockness pens you up inside although
Time keeps chortling as you labor on
To grab it, thus! Oh no! Too bad! It's gone!
You always tick too fast, or else too slow.
But here's your big mistake, Grandpa, right here,
You always chime the same, like this: "Ka-Bong!"
"Ka-Bong!" you say. I say you say that wrong
Unless I hear your desperate, mortal fear:
The pawnshop looms, the landfill calls for you
Unless you do just what I say to do.

Good Provider Loses His Ass at the Chicken Fights
or
How to Write an Apotropaic Poem That Won't Turn Against You

Just don't make the title too long, Diane,
Because there ARE little dancing things,
Who get in your head and make fiery rings,
And leave you in worse shape where you began,
And you can call them devils or just pretend
They ain't there, but, honey, that's crazy,
And doing this job is not for the lazy,
And if the words resist, your work will end.
"Go with the flow," they say, but what do they know
About dodging demons, propitiation
Of imps intent upon annihilation,
And when they have gone, where did they go?
You can't cast a spell if the spell refuses.
Put in the clutch and wait for the Muses.

Another Ha Ha Chuckle for the Blessing of Rest

She thought light would leak on all
True dilemmas, personal honor, life or limb,
What to cook, what to hide from him,
And when she saw some ominous shadow fall
She knew to relish inevitability
Like an old stone statue staring in a tomb,
Silently satisfied in that silent room,
Mutely assimilating shadows she could see.
"My poetry will get you," she wanted to smile,
"My syllabic dynamite, my shapely lines
Of harmony, tangled like wise vines,
Must stack all being in an elegant pile.
But you, O Diogenes, what you are after
Provokes no more than a brief fit of laughter."

Mrs. Alving Contemplates Her Nipples

Hedonism governs men, or simple greed
Deludes them always, so these masculine minds
Delight in lies that their convenience finds
So that for them there's nothing true indeed.
If the lies are just nature's just excretions,
Or by-products of heated oxidation,
I see their value as no more than negation
A healthy memory turns into deletions.
Lusty dudes, braggarts, loud buffoons,
Imploring forgiveness, tender sacrifice,
Though only my surrender will suffice,
I scorn your swaggering, you groveling baboons.
"Mommy! Mommy! Mommy!" these babies cry.
My nipples are mine now. Big babies, good-bye.

Like Epictetus on Mushrooms

If Fortune turns its face toward the sun,
Whose light takes eight minutes to arrive,
Then I put aside impatience to revive
Fortitude in hope when day is done
My sputtering candle may be noted then
For what it's worth, although its little light
Took sixty years of travel through the night
To let its fitful illumination begin.
Duty is useless if no mark is made,
And if the light should vanish, be unseen,
As the Spartan said, I'll fight then in the shade,
Divested of incumbrance, darkly serene.
Take your insincere sympathies, then,
And stick them all elsewhere, all the way in.

The Vigor of Our Cloud-Hidden Friend

"I sang in my chains like the sea."
Dylan Thomas

Let the lyric inside find its way to the sun.
No bonds can prevail when the solstice arrives
And the tide changes. Once it has begun,
The impulse overwhelms and madly drives
Obstacles aside, careening recklessly
Over the gasping ghosts and empties, colliding
Everywhere but always bouncing free,
Charged again by the force of the heart in hiding,
Toward its dream and its awakening
And its calm rest, its last elaboration
And its inevitable, silent beginning,
Simplification and inspiration.
In the end is the word; let this variation
Let the lyric inside find its way to the sun.

Let Decrepitude Run the Table

My old sleepless opponent wants to renew
Our old battle. My copy of *The Art of War*
Has become a dilapidated last stop for
Silverfish, and my dented blades are due
For the junkyard. Like a dozing, aged hound,
I growl in my dreams, demolishing some specter
I once took on, as furious as Hector,
As I drowse in a warm spot, sprawled on the ground.
My *serenatas* now propose to amuse
My small grandchildren; my infrequent passes
By the mirror serve to help me find my glasses,
Through which, when found, I hope to find news
Of comfort. Time, and not my ancient enemy,
Proclaims this gentle victory over me.

Elderly Cassandra Foresees that the Orderly Cleaning Her Backside Will Someday Write Poetry about Waco

Hygiene may have its brief humiliations
But those, as Baudelaire once declared,
Are gifts of God, and if he had dared
To be more specific, these capitulations
Before incontinence grossly lay bare
Odious effusions while the Muses sing
Prophecies of how the future will bring
A new lyric voice to announce everywhere
Divine inspiration will bloom in this city,
And this young man with his diapers and gloves
Will raise a clear voice for the city he loves
And be crowned for both his passion and pity.
Having breathed foulness, may he gladly exhale
The force of the Muses, let purity prevail.

Song of the Cabbage Head

As a newly acknowledged cabbage-head I say
The arrow that nailed old Troilus will miss
More of my crew than amorous folk will kiss.
I laugh a bit at what has gone away.
So, shake hands, O rapturous creation.
The coffee does its work here fairly well,
And I have a treasure house of tales to tell
When silence fails to smother my narration.
You will not see me tie myself in tangles
Or yodel up heartbreak like a youthful swain
Or go on forever about my inner pain,
Beset by love from various dangerous angles.
No, you must realize my responsive ritual
Has evolved toward the vegetable a little.

Mr. Poe Extends a Mexican Invitation

Let there be no blind assurance here
That this page will not gather up itself
And leap at you, wrap you into a taco of death,
Smothering, pressing out all the air
With which you always make such foolish noise
And celebrate misjudgment, crow out loud
Raucus syllables of emptiness, rude hoots
Of lewd confusion, gross gasps of glee.

Keep your paper knife ready, staple gun
Loaded, tactical paper clips ready to reach.
Wisdom is broken, inanimate matter revolts,
The page gathers itself for fatal attack,
Its molecules twitching, its raging words
Cursing complacency: its strength will explode.

Will you need hot sauce? Ha ha! Onions?
Pico de gallo? A little *guacamole*?
Have you been to my graves?
I'll see you quite soon, my friend. *Hasta pronto.*

Academic Couple #1760

He had an appointment with Mr. Poe's ghost
But forgot to write it down. She felt most free
With English ladies of the previous century
Who scribbled their thoughtful novels diligently
And did not like aversions to decency,
Though he liked fake flowers of evil most.
One hopes the Raven forgave the candidate
For missing the appointment and quoting Old Man Frost
And drinking tequila at someone else's cost
And showing up for Latin class abominably late.
We do our best within our dubious trade,
He told himself sincerely, rolling up a joint,
The cards we are dealt are the ones that get played,
And punctuality always misses the point.

Call Me Inconsiderate, Honey

Call me inconsiderate—that is fair;
No denial here, no equivocation,
Stichomythia, or retaliation,
Mock-heroic self-justification,
No, when it happens I am there.
Here, rather, not hiding my masked face
More than necessary, less than well,
Perhaps, if anyone here can tell,
If anyone cares at all in this place.
One has one's own calculus of remorse
Ticking away within. Some honesty
Of conscience feeds it sparingly,
Often rather grudgingly, of course,
Inconsideration guiding me.

Fourteener for the Busy Bee

She thought about that sonnet in the shower,
And she dared it mildly not to behave.
It stalked her to coffee, but she remained brave,
Brandishing her mind to show her own power.
Still, as she gave a clever presentation,
It came at her slyly, a gently-felt distraction,
Promising a bothersome dissatisfaction,
As words she chose brought slight frustration.
She drew her telephone forth from her purse
And googled vocabulary for subtlety,
Almost sure she could nail to a tree
A riddle provoking her heart like a curse.
Oh, let it rest, sister, it's hidden so well
In the fable of love no busy bee can tell.

Troubled Stoic Deletes Favorite Pancake Recipe

Written in the Grease Monkey waiting room on the day after D-Day

Appetite does blindside a drowsy mind
With sweet invitation to treachery,
And morning coffee yearns for company
Of the fragrant hot and buttery kind.
Breakfast with Jezebel? Was I really there,
Breathing breakfast perfume as the sun rose
And shouted, "Now is when the rooster crows!"
And pecan pancake vapor wafted from her hair?
This philosophy generates cheap shots
But economy is our lubrication,
Asking for thrift in imagination,
Mostly functional except in some spots.
Damn, one fights so to say farewell
To sweet pancakes and juicy Jezebel.

Héloïse and Abelard Dissolve in the Student Center Cafeteria

"All nominalists die happy," she wrote,
Smiling at her Schnauzer dog, or cat,
"And happy are the brave, but what is that?
For what is a word but a denotative note?
And courage but a gloss, a pretentious noise?
And death but another otiose claim
Syllable selection empowers us to blame
With *savoir faire*, superior equipoise?"
That's why they parted. One's lowbrow taste
Deemed the other's supercilious perspective
In need of experiential corrective,
But she preferred what she had long embraced.
"What the hell," he whispered to his poodle,
Or, more precisely, his cockadoodle.

Fresh Water Jellyfish Head for the Rapids

No, I didn't think you so much hated me
As wished I were the hell off somewhere
Where few good things ever happen there
And I no longer strangle liberty.
Let me blame shortcomings on my birth,
For Grandpa Jellyfish did fight for the South
And Grandma liked to operate her mouth
Sometimes for what the scolding sound was worth.
And in my childhood several hurricanes
Played hell with slash pines in our yard
And must have made early learning hard
As heavy thunder shook my jiggling brains.
Yet still I dream that irresistible dream
Of turning back and making haste upstream.

Think of it this way, as metaphors, we
Navigate, baubled, one visual flow,
While, parallelwise, in the mind we go
Bobbing and drifting capriciously.
Within our own spheres most concerned,
Inwardly intoxicated, greedily
Absorbing and perceiving, happy to be
With idle pleasures studiously learned
Until unscrolling of the mind declares—
Horresco referens!—blank solitude
Suddenly evicts the sweet interlude
And clotheslines our hero unawares.
Can any reversal on this table
Produce a fitting outcome for this fable?

New Orleans: The Reparations for Prohibition

And to ice the cake,
The House of Representatives
Parades down Canal Street
Blowing tubas and trombones,
In drag, of course, with sequins,
Oom pa, oom pa, oh, mamá!

Age before beauty! We all know
The best revenge is when the good times roll.
And poverty is a kind of wealth,
So says jazz, Socrates, and thongs,
And philosophy with its feet on the ground
Tramples both dead silence and lies,
The two-faced joy of the three-headed dog.
If we must crawfish, ladies and men,
Let's do so with the bluesiest hearts.
Let's hit these carnival streets again.

Prince Myshkin Bets on Being Prepared

"It was the sense you had," she said to me,
"That the curve of the future was full of grace
And experience would be prosperity,
And, in time, all things would fall in place.
That was the problem, for we could see
Those hideous demons of excruciating disgrace
Whooping it up shamefully
To destroy all peace. I rest my case."
And she was right, as fair ladies go,
Her slightly supercilious smile aside,
To set me straight on things all men should know,
Correcting hybris, complacency, and pride.
But while eyes look to purchase what they see,
Behind the back, there may treason be.

Slap That Mosquito, Phaedrus, My Friend

Yeah, we split the atom long ago
Down there in good old Statenville,
With a .22 rifle and some time to kill
We learned everything we needed to know.
The bullfrogs would bellow the whole truth at night,
And the yellow flies' malice harmonized the theme,
While old books drew forth a heavenly dream,
And Plato pranced in the piney-woods light.
Yeah, that Alapaha River cleans itself out
Every ten feet, just as history
Does the same in mind, irrevocably,
The future sunlit, the past in shady doubt.
Here's the flatwoods wisdom. Here's the goods
Straight from the Olympus of the flatwoods.

Roman Mosaic Predicts Texas Cadillac Ranch

"A sonnet is a day's work. Or make that a week."
—Poe

Don't tell me you already know about that.
It was dark and chilly down by the poet's tomb
Behind a church, in shadows and in gloom,
And I stood there, fearfully, and took off my hat,
Feeling that Poe's ghost might croak a command
Like "Beware of alcohol!" or "Leave women alone!"
But there was no such croak, no lonely moan.
It doesn't work that way, I now understand:
He waits to get at you when you're blind,
Distracted by passion, something that draws you in
And erases caution. So you pick up your pen
And there he stands, with that blood-curdling grin,
Paralyzing time and space, all presence of mind,
And says, "All right, son, here I am again."

Sola Scriptura Hits the Home Stretch

> *For Walter M. Gordon, S. J., my friend, who, dying of cancer, asked me to complete the final four pages of his book on a saint.*

The wheels come off the apple cart, and then
Stuff like love, salvation, beauty, integrity,
The Muses' flow of heavenly harmony,
Go rattlingly awry, disordered again.
Now we both agreed that that's how it goes,
No wreaths of laurel then, no delightful rose,
No elegiac fiddles invoking the ages
Or exquisite ladies fingering our pages.
We had a deal, we thought, and on your side
Was old Academia, standing like a wall
Of purple sandstone, justifying all
The humble glories within humanist pride;
On mine, affection for the maverick mind,
For *sola scriptura* and Plato's great game,
On which, at times, our views were the same,
And for music made with whatever we find.
We both taught Shakespeare: you learned from the stage;
I was too long deluded by the page;
But both of us knew what the theater is for,
And I'll never finish your book on St. Thomas More.

Mrs. Collins on Ritual and Routine

Listen, I'm tired of this. You do what you can
And make a fuss about pronouns and liberty
And how your anxious discomfort has to be
The centerpiece of everybody's plan.
Let me be somewhat detached, and then
Some kind tolerance, some patience at least
Will rain on the hell where the jealous demons feast
And cool down the conflict, let peace come again.
If we were saints, our glowing little haloes
Would light up our paths in truth manifest
And leave us no doubt what utterances are best,
But as things stand, neither of us knows.
If I can keep my trap shut, it may be
That tomorrow we'll stumble into felicity.

A Light Blues for Aphasia

You step your light foot
A step toward inaction,
Because when it's heavy,
Oh, there's no traction.

Don't be proud.
Nothing's louder
Than old pride
That blows the tight lid off,
So nothing's left inside.

My good old dog,
With his wise eyes,
Sees my face,
He knows
Something not too very good
Is going on inside.

Oh, aphasia,
Play on so light,
And fade just for me
The favor of flavoring
Your imminent departure
Not just sentimentally
But syncopating a riddling rhythm
For an intrigue, one last subtlety.

Camping in the Rain

Light rain pleases kind meditation,
Erasing traces of crude force and battle,
Rinsing perception of contamination,
And drowning lust's last strangled rattle.
Get the guitar out of the truck and play
Something in tune with this drifting rain:
The Leonard Cohen song you did yesterday,
Or something about the old home and pain,
To fire up a harmonious accord
With light precipitation, which is, after all,
The tears of the gods, and our only reward
For solid fidelity when absolutes fall.
Get that guitar out of the truck and tell
How this wet and weary world has gone to hell.

R. W. Haynes, Professor of English at Texas A&M International University, has published poetry in many journals in the United States and in other countries. As a scholar, he specializes in British Renaissance literature, and he has also taught extensively in such areas as medieval thought, Southern literature, classical poetry, and writing. Since 1992, he has offered regular graduate and undergraduate courses in Shakespeare, as well as seminars in Ibsen, Chaucer, Spenser, rhetoric, and other topics. In 2004, Haynes met Texas playwright/screenwriter Horton Foote and has since become a leading scholar of that author's remarkable oeuvre, publishing a book on Foote's plays in 2010 and editing a collection of essays on his works in 2016. Haynes also writes plays and fiction. In 2016, he received the SCMLA Poetry Award ($500) at the South Central Modern Language Association Conference. Three collections of his poetry have been published, *Laredo Light* (Cyberwit 2019), *Let the Whales Escape* (Finishing Line Press 2019), and *Heidegger Looks at the Moon* (Finishing Line Press 2021).

www.ingramcontent.com/pod-product-compliance
Lightning Source LLC
Chambersburg PA
CBHW030225170426
43194CB00007BA/869